PROPHESY YOUR YEAR OFFICIAL WORKBOOK

THE ADVENTURE OF DISCOVERING GOD'S VOICE THROUGHOUT THE YEAR

LINDSEY REIMAN

DESTINY IMAGE

Destiny Image P.O. Box 310, Shippensburg, PA 17257-0310

This book and all other Destiny Image's books are available at Christian bookstores and distributors worldwide.

For Worldwide Distribution, Printed in the U.S.A.

Reach us on the Internet: www.destinyimage.com.

ISBN 13 TP: 9798881504052

ISBN 13 eBook: 9798881504069

CONTENTS

INTRODUCTION

Welcome to the "Prophesy Your Year Official Workbook," a transformative journey designed to deepen your spiritual awareness and enhance your connection with God through the powerful practice of intentional reflection and prophetic inquiry. As you embark on this journey, you will be guided through a series of thought-provoking prompts and exercises tailored to help you engage with God's voice, uncover His promises, and discover the paths He has laid out for you in the coming year.

KEY TAKEAWAYS FROM THE WORKBOOK

This workbook is built on several foundational principles that are integral to nurturing a vibrant, dynamic relationship with God:

- **Active Engagement with God's Voice**: This workbook encourages you to actively seek and listen to God's voice. Each month, you are invited to engage with a specific prompt that will challenge you to reflect on various aspects of your spiritual and personal life. From understanding the beauty of your race in January to exploring the mysteries of God's plans in December, each prompt is designed to deepen your spiritual insights and foster a responsive dialogue with God.

- **Cultivating a Heart of Reflection**: Reflection is a crucial theme throughout this workbook. You are encouraged to not only answer the prompts but to reflect deeply on how God's answers manifest in your life. This ongoing reflection helps build a bridge between divine guidance and practical application, ensuring that your spiritual journey is both grounded and guided by God's wisdom.

- **Embracing the Full Spectrum of Spiritual Emotions**: Throughout the year, you will explore various emotional landscapes—from gratitude and wonder to dealing with disappointment and seeking divine mysteries. This workbook guides you through these emotions, helping you to understand and process them in a way that strengthens your faith and enriches your spiritual understanding.

- **Documenting Your Spiritual Journey**: As part of this prophetic journey, you are encouraged to document your insights, revelations, and the fulfillment of God's promises. This documentation is vital as it serves as a testament to God's faithfulness and your growth over the year. It also provides a tangible record that you can reflect on in future years, deepening your appreciation for how far you have come.

- **Practical Steps Towards Spiritual Growth**: Each chapter not only offers spiritual insights but also provides practical, actionable steps to apply these insights in your daily life. From cultivating thankfulness to engaging in activities that spark wonder, these steps are designed to help you live out your faith actively and intentionally.

WHAT YOU CAN EXPECT TO RECEIVE

This workbook is designed to transform not just your year but your approach to life and spirituality. Here's what you can expect to receive from your dedicated engagement with this workbook:

- **A Deeper Connection with God**: By consistently seeking God's voice and opening your heart to His guidance, you will experience a deeper, more meaningful relationship with Him.
- **Enhanced Spiritual Awareness**: Through the monthly prompts and the practice of reflection, you will become more attuned to the spiritual dimensions of your life, recognizing God's hand in everyday situations.
- **Personal and Spiritual Growth**: Each exercise is an opportunity to grow personally and spiritually. You will be challenged to expand your understanding, embrace new perspectives, and apply biblical principles more profoundly in your life.
- **A Record of Your Journey**: By the end of the year, you will have a comprehensive record of your conversations with God, insights received, and prayers answered. This record will not only serve as a personal spiritual archive but also as a beacon of encouragement and a source of guidance for the future.

- **Renewed Mindset and Attitudes**: Engaging with this workbook will renew your mindset and transform your attitudes. You will find yourself more open to God's possibilities, more resilient in the face of challenges, and more joyful in your daily walk with God.

As you turn each page and explore each month's focus, remember that this workbook is more than just a guide—it is a companion on your journey to discovering the deeper rhythms of God's grace and the profound mysteries of His plans for you. Embrace each moment, cherish each revelation, and step boldly into the purpose and promise that await you in your prophetic year.

~

CHAPTER 1

JANUARY

Remember, God's guidance often comes in simple whispers that prompt significant changes. Stay open and attentive to His voice, knowing that He speaks to prepare, protect, and propel you into His best for your life.

"Your ears shall hear a word behind you, saying, 'This is the way, walk in it,' Whenever you turn to the right hand or whenever you turn to the left." - Isaiah 30:21 (NKJV)

As we step into a new year, I encourage you to **Begin with Prayer and Inquiry.** Start by asking God what He desires for you to focus on. This approach helps illuminate your path and aligns you with God's plans. **Recording Divine Responses** is crucial; maintaining a journal of these conversations allows you to track and reflect on God's guidance over time.

Understanding whether God's messages are metaphorical or literal is essential in **Interpreting Prophetic Insights**. This discernment can profoundly affect how you receive and act on divine communications. For instance, consider the practice of **Preparation and Order**, as simple directives from God can prepare you for unforeseen challenges, much like the experience shared by Russell, whose organization efforts became critical when facing health issues.

Russell's experience also highlights the **Unexpected Outcomes** of following divine instructions. His seemingly ordinary act of organizing was divinely positioned to help him manage a severe health crisis later. This teaches us the potential significance of every act of obedience to God's word.

Introducing **The Role of Prophetic Acts**, these are not merely symbolic but are acts of faith reflecting spiritual truths. By performing these acts, we bring God's instructions into physical reality, potentially leading to spiritual breakthroughs. From Elisha's arrows to Ezekiel's dramatic representations, **Biblical Examples of Prophetic Acts** show the power of these practices.

Approach prophetic acts with a **Childlike Spirit in Practice** —with joy, wonder, and faith. Whether it's an act as simple as anointing doors or a symbolic march around your home, these actions deepen your spiritual connection. Remember, **Simplicity in Prophetic Acts** is key; they should be straightforward yet profound.

Lastly, always **Engage and Reflect** on how these practices influence your spiritual growth. Keep an open heart and mind, ready to act on the divine revelations you encounter, and continuously reflect on the implications of your actions and God's guidance in your life.

REFLECTIVE QUESTIONS

1. How have you experienced hearing from God in the past, and how can you cultivate a more attentive listening posture this year?
2. Reflect on a time when you felt prompted to act on a seemingly small instruction from God. What was the outcome?
3. In what ways can you incorporate prophetic acts into your daily spiritual practices to enhance your connection with God?
4. How does the concept of approaching God with a childlike spirit change your perception of spiritual obedience?
5. What are some personal examples where you've seen the literal or metaphorical fulfillment of a prophetic word in your life or in the lives of others around you?

ACTIONABLE STEPS

- **Cultivate a Routine of Asking and Listening**: Begin each day by asking God a specific question about what you should focus on or be aware of. Record any insights or impressions you receive in a journal.
- **Equip Yourself with Biblical Examples**: Study the biblical examples of prophetic acts mentioned in the chapter (like those of Elisha and Ezekiel) to understand how they align with the instructions God gives you. This study will help you frame your own actions within a biblical context.

- **Engage in a Prophetic Act**: Choose one prophetic act this month. Approach it with joy and curiosity—whether it's symbolically unlocking a door to new opportunities or taking a literal step forward in faith. Reflect on the spiritual significance of this act and observe any changes or shifts that occur.

Journaling **Prompt**

Reflect and write a letter from God to you, based on what you feel He is asking you to be aware of this month and possibly for the entire year. How do you feel about the instructions or insights given? What actions can you take to align with this prophetic word?

~

CHAPTER 2
FEBRUARY

As you focus on your relationships this February, remember that God is with you in every connection you nurture. He delights in your efforts to strengthen the bonds of love and fellowship.

"A new commandment I give to you, that you love one another; as I have loved you, that you also love one another."
- John 13:34 (NKJV)

This February, we expand our focus beyond romantic love to embrace all types of relationships, acknowledging that **God's Relational Nature** influences every connection. Whether with family, friends, coworkers, or future partners, each relationship deserves our attention and care. By using **Prayer as a Tool for Relationship Growth**, we actively seek God's wisdom on how to strengthen these bonds.

Introducing **Prophetic Acts** into our relationships offers a dynamic way to manifest God's will. These faith-inspired actions, ranging from simple gestures like laying hands on a pillow to stepping out of comfort zones, are grounded in **Person-**

alized Prophetic Words that guide each unique situation. Through these actions, we witness the **Impact of Prophetic Acts** —transformative changes that enhance our relationships and deepen connections.

The chapter uses **Learning from Testimonies** to illustrate the effectiveness of these acts, encouraging us to **Engage and Reflect** on their outcomes. As we consider **Symbolic Prophetic Acts** for our relationships, we are motivated to implement similar practices, ensuring that our interactions are enriched with divine guidance and love.

This month, embrace the opportunity to strengthen every relationship in your life through prayer and prophetic acts, trusting in God's plan to enrich and transform your connections.

REFLECTIVE QUESTIONS

1. How can applying the concept of **God's Relational Nature** enhance your interactions this month?
2. How can **Prayer as a Tool for Relationship Growth** change your approach to a relationship needing attention?
3. What **Prophetic Act** could you perform to bless a specific relationship, and why?
4. How do the testimonies shared demonstrate the impact of **Prophetic Acts** on relationships?
5. How can you align your actions with God's will in your relationships?

ACTIONABLE STEPS

- **Cultivate a Prayer Strategy for Relationships**: Establish a daily prayer routine focusing on different relationships, seeking specific divine guidance for each.
- **Equip Yourself with Scriptural Foundations**: Deepen your understanding of relationships through scripture study, especially those related to prophetic acts.
- **Engage in a Prophetic Act**: Select one relationship to perform a prophetic act for this month, such as expressing appreciation or offering a prayer of blessing.

JOURNALING Prompt

Reflect on your relationships this month. Write about how you can integrate the prophetic insights and actions discussed into these relationships, contemplating what God might be guiding you to do differently to enrich these connections.

CHAPTER 3
MARCH

You are never alone in your journey. God walks alongside you, guiding each step as you inquire of Him. Trust in His promises, and be assured that He is attentive to your heart's cry.

"Trust in the Lord with all your heart, and lean not on your own understanding; in all your ways acknowledge Him, and He shall direct your paths." — Proverbs 3:5-6 (NKJV)

In this chapter, we explore the various pathways through which we, as believers, are called to **march forward in faith**, seeking to align our spiritual, emotional, or physical journeys with the Lord's purpose for our lives. This journey begins by understanding the significance of taking an active role in our spiritual walk. To **march forward in faith** means to move deliberately in the direction that God is leading us, which might be as profound as a call to ministry or as personal as improving our health. Each step forward is a step taken in faith, trusting that God is guiding us through His Spirit.

It's crucial to begin with the right questions. Asking God,

"What am I marching forward toward?" allows us to open up to His divine guidance. The **power of asking** such questions is not to be underestimated; it is through these inquiries that God reveals the directions and actions we are to take. This reflective questioning aligns with the biblical encouragement to seek wisdom, as it is freely given by God to those who ask.

As we proceed on our paths, it becomes important to look out for and **recognize signs from God**. These signs serve as confirmations of our journey's authenticity and alignment with God's will. For example, a recurring theme or symbol in your life might be God's way of speaking directly to you. Recognizing these signs enhances our sensitivity to divine directions and assures us that we are not alone in our journey.

In connecting with God's plan for our lives, it is often helpful to **connect the dots** of seemingly random events or conversations that, upon reflection, reveal a pattern or direction from God. This practice isn't just about finding patterns for the sake of it; it's about seeing the hand of God move in our lives, guiding us gently towards our destiny. This realization can be thrilling and deeply affirming.

Community plays a vital role in our spiritual journeys. The chapter discusses the **importance of community in discerning God's voice**. Often, God will use those around us to speak prophetic words or confirmations that are meant to guide us. These words from our brothers and sisters in Christ can be pivotal in clarifying our path, providing us with assurance or caution as needed.

However, while the community is instrumental, it is also necessary to **judge these prophecies**. Not every word spoken over us is from God. We must use discernment, weighing each prophetic word against the truth of Scripture and the witness of the Holy Spirit within us. This critical engagement ensures that we adhere only to what aligns with God's character and His revealed Word.

An exciting aspect of following God is encouraged to **nurture curiosity**. Rather than always seeking straightforward answers, we should cultivate a sense of wonder about the mysteries of God. This curiosity leads us into deeper relationship with God, as we explore the richness of His revelations and the breadth of His work in our lives and the world.

This chapter also challenges us to **seek out hidden truths**. Like treasure hunters, we are invited to discover the deeper things of God, those He conceals for us to find. This search is not only intellectually fulfilling but spiritually enriching, drawing us closer to the heart of God and His eternal wisdom.

When dealing with prophetic insights, we are taught the value of **metaphorical interpretation**. Instead of taking every prophetic word literally, we should consider them through a symbolic lens. This approach allows for a broader and often more profound understanding of what God might be communicating. It helps us to avoid the pitfalls of misinterpretation, allowing the true meaning of God's messages to unfold in our lives.

Finally, we come to understand that discerning and following God's direction is often a **collective journey**. We are not meant to walk this path alone but are part of a larger body of believers, each contributing different pieces to the same puzzle. As we share our insights and prophecies, we help to build a more complete picture of God's plan for us collectively and individually.

REFLECTIVE QUESTIONS

1. What is the current direction in your spiritual journey, and how can you identify what God is calling you to?
2. How have you experienced God's signs or confirmations in your life recently?
3. In what ways do you engage with your community to discern God's voice together?
4. What prophetic words have you received that you have yet to explore or connect?
5. How can you nurture curiosity in your spiritual life to remain open to God's revelations?

ACTIONABLE STEPS

- **Cultivate: Develop a Habit of Inquiry** Set aside time each week for intentional prayer and inquiry. Ask the Lord specific questions about your life's direction, and listen for His responses.
- **Equip: Build a Prophetic Community** Engage with fellow believers in prophetic prayer sessions or discussion groups where you can share and discern words together. Seek out mentorship from those experienced in prophetic ministry.
- **Engage: Keep a Spiritual Journal** Start a journal dedicated to documenting prophetic words, signs, and personal revelations. Use this journal to track connections and insights over time, creating a record of your spiritual journey.

. . .

JOURNALING Prompt

Reflect on the areas of your life where you are marching forward. What specific actions or decisions are you sensing from the Holy Spirit? Record any signs or confirmations you have received in this process and contemplate how they interconnect.

CHAPTER 4
APRIL

Keep your faith refreshed and your heart open to new growth.
God is continually working in the garden of your soul, nurturing
and tending to areas that are ripe for development. Trust in His
perfect timing and wise care.

**"But grow in the grace and knowledge of our Lord and Savior
Jesus Christ. To Him be the glory both now and forever!
Amen." — 2 Peter 3:18 (NKJV)**

In this chapter, we explore a deeply resonant question for our spiritual and personal growth: "What needs watering?" As we journey through life, often caught up in the rush of day-to-day responsibilities, it's crucial to pause and consider what areas of our lives require nurturing. This question isn't just about identifying needs; it's about engaging in a thoughtful dialogue with the Holy Spirit to discover which aspects of our lives we should focus on to foster growth and health.

When I ask myself, "What needs watering?" I'm really

inquiring about where my attention and efforts should be directed. For some of us, **personal application of watering** might mean tending to relationships that have been strained or neglected—perhaps it's reaching out to a family member or deepening a friendship. For others, it could involve personal development, such as reviving a dormant skill or dedicating time to spiritual study and reflection. The key here is to understand that watering can vary greatly from one person to another, and it's essential to tailor this concept to your own life's conditions and needs.

Asking the right questions is transformative. The **importance of asking the right questions** cannot be overstated—it catalyzes our growth by opening doors to new insights and directions. It transforms simple thoughts into conversations with God about what truly matters in our growth as followers of Christ. This process of inquiry is foundational in developing a more intimate and responsive relationship with God, where we learn to listen and respond to His gentle guidance.

Recognizing signs from God in response to our questions about what needs watering helps in affirming our path and sharpening our focus. For instance, if you've been contemplating whether to dedicate more time to spiritual disciplines, and suddenly you come across multiple messages or sermons on this topic, take it as a **recognizing sign** from God. These signs serve as confirmations that help steer our actions and reassure us of His presence in our decision-making processes.

In this search for direction, patterns in our experiences and interactions play a crucial role. These **patterns as divine communication** can appear as repeated themes in our conversations, recurring thoughts during prayer, or consistent messages across different mediums which all point towards a specific area or topic. Such patterns are not coincidental; they are often God's way of drawing our attention to something significant, reinforcing His message through multiple witnesses as stated in 2 Corinthians 13:1.

The **role of community in discernment** is another aspect we delve into in this chapter. Our spiritual brothers and sisters can provide not only support but also perspective that might be missing from our own interpretations. Engaging with our community allows us to benefit from the collective wisdom and spiritual sensitivity of the group, which can be incredibly affirming as we seek to understand what needs more attention in our lives.

Sometimes, the insights we receive from others can take the form of **prophetic words**. These **prophetic words** can act as direct messages from God concerning areas in our lives that require attention. Whether it's a call to renew our focus on family, a nudge towards a neglected project, or a push towards personal healing, these words can powerfully affirm and direct our actions.

However, it's also important to approach this process with **patience in seeing signs**. Not all confirmations are immediate. Sometimes, it takes time for God's signs to manifest in our lives. This period of waiting is not a passive time; it's a dynamic state of expectancy and trust in God's timing, which often teaches us as much about faith as it does about the specific areas we are focusing on.

Moreover, there is profound value in **living in mystery**, in not having all the answers, and in being open to the unexpected ways God may choose to speak to us. This stance requires humility and a deep trust in God's sovereignty, recognizing that we walk by faith, not by sight.

Lastly, I encourage you to **document insights and patterns** that emerge as you contemplate what needs watering. Keeping a journal or a record can help you trace God's hand over your life, providing a tangible reminder of His faithfulness and guidance.

This documentation becomes a personal testament to the ways God moves in your life, helping you remember His goodness and encouraging you to remain attentive to His whispers.

REFLECTIVE QUESTIONS

1. What area of your life do you feel has been neglected or needs more of your attention this month?
2. How can you apply the concept of watering in a personal way that resonates with your current spiritual or emotional needs?
3. What patterns have you noticed in your life that might be God trying to communicate something important to you?
4. In what ways can your faith community help you discern and focus on areas that need watering?
5. How do you handle periods of waiting for signs or confirmations from God?

ACTIONABLE STEPS

- **Cultivate: Regular Reflection**
- Cultivate a habit of regular reflection by setting aside time each day to meditate on the question, "What needs watering?" Use this time to pray and listen for God's guidance.
- **Equip: Engage with Scripture**
- Equip yourself with scriptural knowledge by studying Bible passages that relate to growth, nurturing, and attention. Reflect on how these

scriptures apply to the areas of your life that you feel need watering.

- **Engage: Community Interaction**
- Engage with your faith community by sharing your insights and asking for feedback on areas you feel need attention. Use community resources to gain different perspectives and support.

JOURNALING **Prompt**

Reflect on the question, "What needs watering in my life?" Journal about the areas you identify and the signs or patterns that might be pointing you towards them. Consider how you can actively nurture these areas over the next month.

CHAPTER 5
MAY

Explore the landscape of your life; see where beauty has grown and where it is yet to bloom. God crafts beauty in every season of our lives, revealing His glory and drawing us closer to Him.

"He has made everything beautiful in its time. Also, He has put eternity in their hearts, except that no one can find out the work that God does from beginning to end." —
Ecclesiastes 3:11 (NKJV)

In this chapter, we explore a deeply resonant theme for May: discovering the beauty that God has planted in our lives. Whether in the laughter of friends, the peace of quiet moments, or the resilience found in overcoming challenges, beauty surrounds us. It's about recognizing these moments and understanding their significance in the tapestry of our spiritual journey.

When I reflect on the idea of **Exploring the Concept of Beauty**, I'm reminded that beauty extends far beyond what meets the eye. It's found in the growth that comes from adversity, the harmony of a community working together, and the silent workings of nature—each element a reflection of God's creativity and care. This month challenges us to look deeper and appreciate the beauty in all aspects of our lives, not just those traditionally acknowledged as beautiful.

The biblical story of the Queen of Sheba's visit to King Solomon illustrates the **power of beauty** in a profound way. It wasn't merely Solomon's wisdom that left an impression; it was the beauty of his court—the order, the attire of the servants, the meticulous arrangements. This story prompts us to consider how we might reflect God's beauty in our own environments, influencing others to recognize and praise God through what they observe in our lives.

Additionally, beauty isn't just something to observe; it's also something to experience and create. Recognizing that **External Beauty as a Reflection of God's Glory** can be a powerful witness to others, we are called to create and maintain beauty in our surroundings as a testament to the Creator. This can be a transformative practice, turning ordinary spaces into testimonies of faith.

Finding Beauty in Trials teaches us that our most challenging moments often lead to the greatest growth. Looking back on difficulties with the perspective of time reveals how such periods have shaped us, molding our character and faith. This aligns with the promise in Isaiah 61:3, where God promises to give beauty for ashes, transforming our trials into triumphs.

This month, take the opportunity to see **God as the Creator of Beauty** in the world around you. This might be through a renewed interest in nature, art, or the simple beauty of daily life. Recognizing God's hand in the seemingly ordinary aspects of the world can deepen our appreciation of His presence and creativity.

As we embrace the various forms of beauty, we learn to

Appreciate Beauty in All Forms—the tangible and intangible, the grand and the simple. This broadens our perspective and enriches our spiritual walk, as we learn to see God's hand in all things, understanding that everything He creates has purpose and value.

Using beauty as a **Conversation Starter with God** this month can lead us to unexpected and enriching spiritual discoveries. Asking God to reveal the beauty in each day invites ongoing dialogue that deepens our relationship with Him, opening our eyes to His continuous work in our lives.

Sometimes, **Prophetic Insights on Beauty** can shift our understanding and appreciation of our circumstances. Engaging with God about the beauty in each month may reveal insights about ourselves and His plans for us, reshaping our perspective and helping us to embrace even the hidden beauty in challenging times.

The encouragement to **Learn from Others' Perceptions of Beauty**, such as in the shared testimonies within our community, shows us the varied ways God communicates and manifests beauty to different people. These stories can inspire us to seek and acknowledge the beauty in our own lives that we might have overlooked.

Lastly, understanding our **Identity and Beauty** reminds us that how we perceive and create beauty is deeply connected to who we are in Christ. Embracing our identity as God's creation allows us to live out our divine purpose, reflecting His beauty in everything we do.

REFLECTIVE QUESTIONS

1. In what ways have you experienced beauty in unexpected situations or challenges in your life?

2. How does the story of Solomon and the Queen of Sheba inspire you to think about beauty in your own environment?

3. What are some aspects of God's creation that you find particularly beautiful, and how do they enhance your understanding of God?

4. How can you use beauty as a tool to lead others to appreciate or praise God?

5. Reflect on a past trial: How can you now see beauty in what was once a difficult situation?

ACTIONABLE STEPS

- **Cultivate: Daily Appreciation of Beauty**
- Cultivate a habit of recognizing beauty daily, whether in nature, interactions with others, or personal achievements. Keep a journal to note these moments of beauty, enhancing your awareness and appreciation.
- **Equip: Study Biblical Examples of Beauty**
- Equip yourself with knowledge by studying biblical instances where beauty played a significant role in spiritual lessons or revelations, such as in the stories of Solomon or the transformation of places and people in the Bible.
- **Engage: Create Beauty**
- Engage in activities that create beauty, whether through art, gardening, writing, or other forms of creative expression. Use these acts of creation as forms of worship and as ways to inspire others to see God's beauty in the world around them.

. . .

Journaling Prompt

Reflect on the question, "Where is the beauty in this month for me?" Consider both the tangible and intangible aspects of beauty you encounter. Journal about how recognizing and appreciating these elements can impact your spiritual journey and daily life.

CHAPTER 6
JUNE

Embrace the truth that God delights in you, not just as His creation, but as a cherished child. He finds joy in who you are, just as you are.

"For you are God's masterpiece, created in Christ Jesus to do good works, which God prepared in advance for us to do." — Ephesians 2:10 (NKJV)

In this chapter, we delve into the profound understanding of our identity in Christ and how it manifests in our daily lives. A foundational aspect of this journey is grasping the truth that God does not only love us, He delights in us. Embracing this **Foundational Truth of God's Delight in Us** transforms our interactions with God, ourselves, and others. It reassures us that our value is not based on our accomplishments or failures but is inherent because of Christ's sacrifice for us.

When I encourage you to explore who you are, I am inviting you to embark on a quest to understand your **Exploring Identity in Christ.** This is not about what you do or the roles you play; it's about who you are at your core—your values, your beliefs, and how these align with God's word. This understanding is crucial as it influences every decision and action you undertake. Knowing who you are in God provides a stable foundation for all aspects of life.

Each of us operates in various capacities throughout different seasons of our lives, much like I did when I was **Operational Identity** as The Disruptor. This month, take the time to reflect on how you are currently expressing your identity in Christ through your actions, decisions, and interactions.

A practical way to affirm your identity is to look back at **God's Previous Affirmations**. Recall the times God has spoken into your life through scripture, prophetic words, or through the encouragement of others. These moments are not random; they are part of a divine pattern that confirms your identity and calling.

Keeping track of these affirmations helps us recognize **Tracking Patterns in Prophetic Words**. By noting recurring themes or messages, we can discern what God is emphasizing in our lives. These patterns often highlight strengths we should develop further or areas God is preparing us to step into.

Asking God for a **Confirmation Through Signs** is another way to solidify your understanding of your identity. Whether it's a specific scripture that comes up repeatedly, a word from a friend that resonates deeply, or an opportunity that aligns perfectly with your skills, these signs can serve as confirmations from God that you are on the right path.

Approaching our identity with **Childlike Wonder** allows us to accept and celebrate our identity joyfully. Like children who marvel at the simple joys of life, we too can find delight in discovering more about who we are and how wonderfully God has made us. This approach keeps our journey of self-discovery light and filled with joy.

This month is also about the **Celebration of Identity**. Each insight into who you are in Christ is a cause for celebration. Recognizing and appreciating how God is using you can boost your confidence and deepen your commitment to live out your divine purpose.

To deepen this understanding, I recommend **Engaging in Spiritual Practices** that reinforce your identity. Whether it's through prayer, worship, fasting, or studying the Bible, these disciplines help cement your identity in Christ and equip you to stand firm against any identity challenges that may come your way.

Lastly, do not underestimate the power of community. **Reflecting on Identity Through Community** helps you see yourself through the eyes of those who know you well. The feedback and insights from your church family or small group can provide external affirmation of your internal journey and help clarify how others witness Christ in you.

Reflective Questions

1. How do you currently perceive God's delight in you, and how does this affect your self-view?
2. In what ways are you seeking to understand your identity in Christ this month?
3. What patterns have you noticed in prophetic words or themes in your life that may be speaking to your current identity in God?
4. What signs have you asked for or received that confirm your understanding of your identity in Christ?
5. How can celebrating every aspect of your identity

enhance your spiritual journey and relationship with God?

- **Cultivate: Daily Affirmations of Identity**
- Cultivate a daily practice of affirming your identity in Christ through scriptural declarations and prayer. Focus on scriptures that speak to who you are in God, reinforcing your sense of divine worth and purpose.
- **Equip: Study and Reflection**
- Equip yourself by studying characters in the Bible who underwent significant identity transformations, such as Gideon or Paul. Reflect on their stories and draw parallels to your own journey of identity in Christ.
- **Engage: Community Feedback**
- Engage actively with your faith community by sharing your journey of understanding your identity. Seek feedback and prophetic insights that can help clarify and affirm how you are to operate in your identity this month.

JOURNALING Prompt

Reflect on the question, "How am I operating in my identity in Christ this month?" Consider the roles, responsibilities, or attributes you are embodying that reflect your understanding of who you are in God. Journal about these reflections and how they align with God's perspective and delight in you.

CHAPTER 7
JULY

Celebrate more, because being alive is in itself a grand
celebration of God's magnificent creation.

**"Let everything that has breath praise the Lord. Praise the
Lord!" - Psalm 150:6 (NKJV)**

In the journey of faith, we often seek grand signs and
miracles as affirmations of God's presence in our lives. Yet,
there is profound divinity in the simplicity and smallness
of everyday moments. Imagine a seer prophet, known for his
spiritual depth, encountering a simple piece of glitter on his
finger while at a restaurant. This man, who has had vivid experiences with angels and even glimpses of Heaven, found himself
captivated by something as small as glitter. This moment
reminds us of the **Encounter with the Divine** that can happen
anytime and anywhere, teaching us to be open to God's presence
in all aspects of life, regardless of their grandeur.

This episode beautifully illustrates **Childlike Wonder**. The
prophet's reaction mirrors how children react to the world—

with pure joy and without skepticism. This type of wonder is vital for us as believers. It keeps our faith fresh and enthusiastic, helping us to maintain a vibrant connection with God. It's about celebrating God's presence in every aspect of our lives, even in those that seem mundane or trivial. When we approach life with such wonder, we find joy in the ordinary, seeing each day anew through a lens of spiritual vitality.

And so, this brings us to the **Simplicity of Faith**. Faith doesn't always require monumental signs to be affirmed; it can be nurtured through the smallest of gestures and moments that we often overlook. Like the glitter on the prophet's finger, these small tokens can be powerful reminders of God's intimate involvement in our lives. They encourage us to keep our hearts open to the divine touches that grace our everyday experiences.

Furthermore, we're called to **Celebrate Small Moments**. Often, we reserve celebration for life's big victories or answers to grand prayers. However, what if we chose to also celebrate the seemingly insignificant successes or the simple answers to prayers? Doing so can transform our everyday experiences into a continuous acknowledgment of God's goodness and provision, fostering a constant state of gratitude and happiness.

By **Approaching with Joy**, we align ourselves with the heart of God. Just as children show excitement and happiness for the small discoveries they make, so too should we rejoice in our daily spiritual discoveries. This joy is not just beneficial for our spiritual lives; it enriches our overall well-being, making our journey with God a delightful adventure rather than a series of tasks or challenges.

The **Impact of Minor Blessings** can be profound. They serve as gentle reminders that God is always with us, guiding and interacting with us in ways that might initially seem insignificant but are, in fact, laden with spiritual significance. Recognizing these blessings can bolster our faith, especially during times when God seems silent or distant.

In celebrating every moment, we are essentially **Living Fully in God's Creation**. Our very existence is a part of the grand celebration of life that God has orchestrated. Each breath we take is a gift, and each day is a new canvas on which God paints His grace and love. Recognizing this can transform our perspective, helping us to live more fully and gratefully.

As we expand our spiritual practices, we should strive to **Expand Our Spiritual Perception**. This means not only seeking God in the extraordinary but also tuning our senses to perceive Him in the ordinary—every smile, every kind gesture from a stranger, every peaceful moment can be a medium of His messages to us.

In this journey, we are encouraged to actively **Seek God's Voice**. Whether He reveals something monumental, like a new career path or a significant life decision, or something as simple as how to have a peaceful conversation with a family member, each is a cause for celebration. His voice adds depth and direction to our lives, guiding us gently towards our divine purpose.

Finally, remember, our presence on this earth is no accident. **Recognizing Our Divine Selection** means understanding that we are here because God chose us to be here. We are part of His divine narrative, created purposefully by a God who knows the end from the beginning. This realization should fill us with a profound sense of purpose and joy as we navigate the complexities of life.

REFLECTIVE QUESTIONS

1. What are the small signs of God's presence you have noticed in your daily life that you typically overlook?
2. How can adopting a childlike wonder change your perspective on spirituality and daily living?
3. In what ways can you celebrate the mundane parts of your life to cultivate a deeper appreciation for God's gifts?
4. How might your spiritual life change if you consciously celebrated both your big and small victories as divine blessings?
5. Reflect on a time when a minor blessing had a major impact on your faith. What was the blessing and how did it affect you?

ACTIONABLE STEPS

- **Cultivate a Habit of Noticing**: Begin each day by writing down one small thing you noticed that made you feel connected to God. This could be as simple as the warmth of the sun or a peaceful moment of silence.
- **Equip Yourself with Knowledge**: Study the biblical figures who experienced God in the mundane, such as Moses and the burning bush, to understand how regular encounters with God shaped their faith and decisions.
- **Engage in Expressive Gratitude**: Make it a practice to share your daily finds with a community or a journal. Expressing gratitude can enhance your

awareness of God's ongoing work in your life and encourage others to notice the same in their lives.

Journaling **Prompt**

Reflect on the ordinary moments this past month where you felt a touch of God's presence. How did these moments influence your feelings of gratitude and your perception of God's involvement in your life? Write about these instances and how they might guide you to notice and celebrate more of such moments.

CHAPTER 8

AUGUST

Celebrate the beginnings and endings as God's orchestrated
movements in your life.

**"To everything there is a season, A time for every purpose
under heaven." - Ecclesiastes 3:1 (NKJV)**

In our lives, we encounter numerous beginnings and endings, each orchestrated by God with divine timing and purpose. Recognizing that **Divine Timing** governs our experiences can profoundly alter how we view these transitions. Every phase, whether a beginning or an ending, fits perfectly into a greater plan designed for our growth and God's glory.

Many of us struggle with endings; we cling to the familiar, fearing what comes next. However, I've learned that **Embracing Endings** is essential for personal and spiritual growth. This realization hit me profoundly after moving back from Redding, California, to Los Angeles. I found that the city had changed, the people had changed, but most importantly, I had changed. I could no longer fit into my old life because it simply did not exist anymore. This taught me to let go of the past and make room for new experiences, highlighting the importance of closures to make way for new chapters.

As we close old chapters, we also encounter **Welcoming New Beginnings**. These are not just times to start afresh but are ripe with opportunities for profound personal transformation and blessings. For instance, when I embraced the end of my time in Los Angeles and began a new chapter elsewhere, it opened doors to unexpected blessings and new paths that aligned better with who I had become.

The essence of **Personal Transformation** is often triggered by such significant life changes. Whether it's a change in location, career, or relationships, these shifts can transform us so deeply that reverting to our 'old self' becomes impossible. We emerge from these transitions fundamentally altered, ready to engage with the world in new ways.

It is also vital to **Seek God's Voice** during these periods of change. By actively praying and seeking God's guidance on what is ending and what is beginning, we align ourselves more closely with His will. This practice not only provides clarity but also comforts us, knowing we are moving in the right direction.

Sometimes, God's adjustments in our lives involve **Low-Stakes Changes**. These might seem minor, like changing a daily routine or abandoning a comforting but distracting habit, but they hold significant spiritual implications. For example, when God asked me to stop using TV as background noise and seek His presence for comfort instead, it deepened my relationship with Him significantly.

This new depth in my relationship with God enhanced my ability to **Listen for Comfort** in His presence rather than in worldly comforts. Replacing superficial soothers with time spent in prayer and meditation has strengthened my faith and reliance on God's provision and peace.

Engaging with the prophetic has also opened my eyes to the precision of **Prophetic Insights** in guiding our steps into the future. Hearing accurate prophecies about my life, such as unexpected speaking engagements that came to fruition, has reinforced my belief in the specific and mindful nature of God's plan for each of us.

Through all these experiences, I've learned the value of **Risk and Faith**. Stepping into the unknown requires courage and a deep trust in God's plan. These risks, whether big or small, are steps of faith that lead us to miraculous discoveries and divine destinations.

Lastly, maintaining a **Continuous Conversation** with God is crucial. This ongoing dialogue where we pour out our fears, celebrate our joys, and share our desires keeps our relationship with Him vibrant and alive. He starts the conversation with His purpose for us and ensures it leads to a fulfilling conclusion in His perfect timing.

In summary, every transition you face is an opportunity to deepen your faith, broaden your horizons, and refine your purpose. Embrace each beginning and ending as a sacred component of your life's divine choreography. Trust in God's timing, for it is impeccable, and remember that with Him, every end is just the start of a new and glorious beginning.

REFLECTIVE QUESTIONS

1. What recent ending in your life might be making way for a new beginning?
2. How can you practice listening to God more intently during times of transition?
3. What small change might God be asking you to make

that could have a significant impact on your spiritual growth?

4. Can you recall a time when an unexpected change led to a surprising and beneficial outcome?
5. How does recognizing the seasonality of life help you cope with changes?

ACTIONABLE STEPS

- **Cultivate Awareness of Seasons**: Keep a journal to record changes and seasons in your life. Reflect on these periodically to understand God's timing and His purposes behind these changes.
- **Equip Yourself with Patience**: Develop patience through meditation on Scriptures that discuss God's timing and purpose (Ecclesiastes 3, Jeremiah 29:11). This can help ground your reactions to changes.
- **Engage in Prayer for Direction**: Regularly set aside time to pray specifically about what is ending in your life and what might be beginning. Seek clarity and peace from God to navigate these transitions confidently.

JOURNALING Prompt

Reflect on a significant ending or beginning in your life from the past year. How did you see God's hand in this event? Write about how this experience has affected your faith and your view of God's timing and purpose.

CHAPTER 9

SEPTEMBER

Embrace the opportunity to deepen your relationship with God by intentionally scheduling time to be with Him.

"Draw near to God and He will draw near to you." - James 4:8 (NKJV)

This month, I encourage you to consider your relationship with God as one of the most treasured relationships in your life, deserving the same, if not more, **Intentionality in Relationship** as relationships with your closest friends or family. Imagine setting a date with God, not out of obligation but from a desire to deepen that sacred connection. This act of scheduling time with God is about creating a space to actively **Listen for God's Voice**. It's about quieting our minds and opening our hearts to hear what He has to say, making these moments not just a ritual but a vital part of our spiritual growth.

During these times, we engage in **Writing as a Spiritual Practice**, where we document the insights and messages received. This writing serves as a tangible reminder of our spiritual path and commitments. It's a practice that not only helps in retaining the messages but also in clarifying our thoughts and reflections on the divine guidance received.

Life doesn't always go as planned, and here, the **Flexibility in Spiritual Practices** plays a key role. Should unexpected events occur, understanding that it's okay to reschedule our date with God without feeling guilty is crucial. This flexibility helps maintain the lightness and joy of our relationship with Him, ensuring that our spiritual life adapts to our everyday living without becoming a burden.

Furthermore, as we walk this path, we find opportunities to **Share Our Faith with Others**, much like Brittany did at the wedding. Sharing these moments of divine interaction can profoundly impact others, demonstrating the living reality of God's presence in our lives. This openness not only strengthens our faith but also invites others to explore their spiritual paths.

By recognizing and **Celebrating Spiritual Milestones**, such as the appearance of shooting stars at just the right moment, we acknowledge and rejoice in the personal and intimate ways God communicates with us. These moments are significant markers in our spiritual journey, affirming God's active presence and care.

Moreover, **Risk-Taking in Faith** and the willingness to share our experiences, even in non-traditional or secular settings, showcases the dynamic and living nature of our faith. These acts of bravery can lead to awe-inspiring moments that reinforce our belief and may even encourage others to seek a similar connection with the divine.

Such interactions are essential for **Witnessing to Nonbelievers**, as they allow us to use our personal experiences and the evident hand of God in our lives to engage others in meaningful dialogue about faith and spirituality.

Consistently scheduling these times emphasizes the importance of **Scheduled Spiritual Intimacy** with God. This dedicated time is as crucial as any important appointment, reflecting our commitment to and valuation of our relationship with God.

In these moments, we often see **God's Faithfulness in Small Details**, which reassures us of His involvement and interest in our lives. Whether it's a timely word or an unexpected blessing, these details underscore His attentiveness and intentionality in His relationship with us.

In summary, by making time for these divine rendezvous, we not only honor God but also enrich our spiritual lives. These intentional meetings with God are not mere entries in our calendar but vibrant encounters that deepen our understanding of Him and strengthen our faith.

REFLECTIVE QUESTIONS

1. How can setting a specific date with God change your relationship with Him?
2. What are some ways you can prepare yourself to listen deeply to God during your scheduled time?
3. How has documenting your spiritual experiences affected your faith journey?
4. Can you think of a time when being flexible in your spiritual practices helped you maintain peace and joy?
5. How might you use your personal testimonies to engage nonbelievers in conversations about faith?

ACTIONABLE STEPS

- **Cultivate a Routine**: Set a regular schedule to meet with God, treating these times as sacred appointments that are as important as any other meeting in your life.
- **Equip Yourself with Tools**: Have a journal dedicated to these dates with God. Use it to write down thoughts, scriptures, prayers, and what you feel God is communicating during your time together.
- **Engage in Sharing**: Look for opportunities to share the insights and experiences from your dates with God with friends, family, or even on social media. This not only affirms your experience but also encourages others to seek similar encounters.

JOURNALING Prompt

Reflect on your most recent date with God. What did you learn about Him and yourself during this time? How did this experience deepen your relationship with God, and what steps can you take to ensure these dates continue to be a meaningful part of your spiritual life?

CHAPTER 10
OCTOBER

Embrace every opportunity as a chance to learn; God often teaches us through the most unexpected experiences.

"If any of you lacks wisdom, let him ask of God, who gives to all liberally and without reproach, and it will be given to him." - James 1:5 (NKJV)

In this journey of faith and life, embracing **Lifelong Learning as a Spiritual Practice** is not just beneficial—it's essential. Learning enriches our souls, sharpens our minds, and deepens our relationship with God. It transcends traditional academic settings, infusing every aspect of our lives with the potential for growth and enlightenment. Each day presents a new opportunity to learn something valuable, not just through books but through every experience and interaction.

Central to our ability to learn effectively is **Humility**. This fundamental trait opens the door to true knowledge and wisdom. It allows us to admit that we don't have all the answers and that there is always room for growth. This posture of humility makes us teachable and receptive to new insights, whether they come from God, the people around us, or the situations we face. Embracing humility is not a sign of weakness but of great strength and wisdom.

Being **Actively Engaged** in seeking out learning opportunities is crucial. It's about more than passive absorption; it's about actively searching for lessons in both the mundane and the extraordinary moments of life. Whether it's a quiet prompt from the Holy Spirit reminding us of a childhood lesson or a challenging problem at work, every moment is ripe with potential for learning.

One of the most profound ways God speaks to us is in the everyday. **Listening for God's Voice** in everyday moments involves tuning into those subtle hints and nudges that can often go unnoticed. Perhaps it's a recurring theme in conversations, a passage of Scripture that stands out, or even a memory that suddenly seems relevant. Paying attention to these details can reveal God's guidance and wisdom in surprising ways.

Documenting Spiritual Insights is a practical tool in our learning arsenal. By writing down what we learn, especially the insights we gain from our relationship with God, we create a lasting record of our spiritual growth. This practice helps us remember the lessons learned and provides a clear path forward, allowing us to revisit and reflect on God's teachings in our lives.

Life is unpredictable, and learning requires **Flexibility**. We must be adaptable in how we receive and integrate new knowledge, understanding that God's lessons can come from anywhere and may require us to step outside our comfort zones.

As we accumulate knowledge and wisdom, it's important to **Share Knowledge with Others**. Sharing what we've learned isn't just about teaching; it's about communing, connecting, and often, it provides a way to solidify our own understanding. This communal aspect of learning can take many forms, from informal discussions with friends to more structured teaching settings.

Preparation for Unexpected Opportunities can often make the difference between fumbling through a situation and handling it with grace. Much like remembering the etiquette of silverware settings at a formal dinner in London, being prepared allows us to handle **Unexpected Opportunities** with grace and confidence, showing God's provision in our preparedness.

Learning from Secular Sources also plays a vital role in our spiritual and personal development. God can use secular sources to teach us important lessons. Whether it's through a YouTube video on etiquette or a book on leadership, we can find valuable insights that are applicable to our spiritual and personal lives.

Finally, maintaining a mindset of **Continuous Inquiry and Reflection** ensures that we never stagnate. Regularly asking ourselves what we're learning and how we can apply it keeps our spiritual journey dynamic and progressive. This ongoing inquiry not only fuels our growth but also keeps our relationship with God active and engaged.

REFLECTIVE QUESTIONS

1. In what areas of your life is God currently encouraging you to learn?
2. How can embracing humility enhance your ability to learn from God and others?
3. What recent insight or lesson have you documented, and how has it impacted your faith?
4. How can you incorporate flexibility in your learning to better respond to God's teachings?
5. How might you use your learning experiences to encourage and teach others in your community?

. . .

Actionable Steps

- **Cultivate a Habit of Daily Reflection**: Set aside time each day to reflect on what you have learned from God, jotting down insights and any actions you might take as a result.
- **Equip Yourself with Diverse Resources**: Gather books, videos, podcasts, and other resources on topics God is leading you to explore. This equips you with the tools to gain a broad understanding of these subjects.
- **Engage in Community Learning**: Share your learning journey with a small group or community. This engagement not only deepens your insights but also helps others in their spiritual growth.

Journaling Prompt

Reflect on a recent learning experience where you felt God was teaching you something vital. How did this lesson come about, and what impact has it had on your understanding of God's character and your personal growth? Write about how this experience has shaped your approach to new learning opportunities.

~

CHAPTER 11

NOVEMBER

Trust in God's goodness and lean into the mystery of His ways, finding joy and thankfulness in both the seen and unseen.

"Be anxious for nothing, but in everything by prayer and supplication, with thanksgiving, let your requests be made known to God." - Philippians 4:6 (NKJV)

In our spiritual journey, confronting the **Fear of Disappointment** is pivotal. Many of us hesitate to look forward with hope because we fear being let down. Yet, embracing this month's prompt to ask, "What will I be thankful for by the time this month rolls around?" is an exercise in bold faith. This question invites us to peer into the future with anticipation, laying our fears aside and trusting in God's promises. It taps directly into our anxieties but also offers a path to overcome them by focusing on potential joys and blessings.

The **Value of Mystery** in our faith journey is profound. It teaches us that not all answers are readily available, and not all paths are clearly marked. This mystery is not a barrier to our faith but an invitation to deeper trust and reliance on God. It encourages us to believe that even in the absence of clarity, God's plans are unfolding for our good. Engaging with this mystery can strengthen our faith, as it requires us to believe in God's goodness despite not seeing the full picture.

Thankfulness as a Spiritual Discipline involves more than just gratitude for blessings received; it is also about maintaining a hopeful anticipation for what is to come. This discipline shapes how we perceive our current circumstances and our future, fostering a mindset that actively looks for God's hand in every situation. By practicing thankfulness, we open our hearts to recognize and appreciate God's influence in all aspects of our lives, both seen and unseen.

Documenting Anticipated Blessings is a powerful practice. When we write down what we hope to be thankful for, we engage in an act of faith. This documentation not only serves as a future reminder of our hopeful expectations but also as a testament to God's faithfulness when we look back. It allows us to "read" our fears and hopes and to confront them with a spiritual perspective that is anchored in God's promises.

Emotional Honesty in Spirituality is crucial. It is important to allow ourselves to feel and express our emotions—whether they are fears, disappointments, or joys—authentically before God. This honesty deepens our relationship with Him and enhances our spiritual well-being, providing a clearer path to understanding and peace.

Through **Regular Reflection on Progress**, we can observe how our perspectives shift over time. This reflection is not just about acknowledging what God has done but also about understanding how we have grown in our capacity to trust and be thankful. It helps adjust our expectations and enhances our ability to remain thankful through varying circumstances.

A **Teachable Spirit** and openness to growth are essential

traits for anyone seeking to deepen their understanding of God and themselves. Being teachable means we are always ready to learn, willing to adjust our understandings, and eager to embrace new insights that God may reveal along our path.

Sharing Testimonies of Faith with others not only reinforces our own faith but also kindles hope and encouragement in the community around us. When we share how we are anticipating God's blessings and how we have seen His work in our lives, we spread the spirit of thankfulness and faith.

Cultivating Hope in Uncertainty is a vital strategy for maintaining a positive outlook. It enables us to face the unknown with a confident expectation of God's goodness, regardless of our current situations. This hope is not passive; it is an active, powerful stance that influences our emotional and spiritual health.

Finally, a deep **Recognition of God's Sovereignty** underpins our ability to be truly thankful. When we acknowledge that God's ways are higher than our ways, we can rest in the assurance that every aspect of our lives is under His wise and loving control. This recognition frees us from the need for complete understanding and allows us to trust in His perfect plan.

By embracing these principles, we not only cultivate a richer, more fulfilling spiritual life but also equip ourselves to handle life's uncertainties with grace and confidence. Each lesson learned, each moment of thankfulness, and each step taken in faith brings us closer to the heart of God, where true joy and peace reside.

REFLECTIVE QUESTIONS

1. What fears of disappointment might be hindering your ability to be thankful for future blessings?

2. How can embracing the mystery of God's plans enhance your faith and spiritual growth?
3. What blessings are you anticipating, and how are you documenting these expectations?
4. How does emotional honesty impact your spiritual health and relationship with God?
5. In what ways can you cultivate a teachable spirit to better learn from your experiences?

ACTIONABLE STEPS

- **Cultivate a Practice of Anticipation**: Start each day by writing down something you are hopeful for or something you are asking God to bring into your life. This practice encourages a proactive stance towards thankfulness.

- **Equip Yourself with Tools for Emotional Expression**: Keep a journal specifically for spiritual reflections, including your fears, joys, disappointments, and hopes. This will help you process your emotions healthily and constructively.

- **Engage in Community Sharing**: Regularly share your journey of thankfulness with a trusted friend or a spiritual group. This engagement not only provides support but also multiplies the joy as you witness God working not just in your life but in others' lives as well.

Journaling Prompt

Reflect on a time when you felt disappointed by unmet expectations. How did you handle those feelings? Write about how this experience could help you approach future uncertainties with hope and thankfulness, trusting in the mystery of God's perfect plan.

CHAPTER 12

DECEMBER

Keep your heart open to wonder, as it leads us closer to God and
deepens our appreciation of life.

**"You will seek Me and find Me when you search for Me with
all your heart." - Jeremiah 29:13 (NKJV)**

As we journey through life, the **Importance of Wonder**
cannot be overstated. It's a profound force that
Enhances Curiosity and fuels our desire to explore
both our world and our faith more deeply. Wonder opens our
eyes to the miracles of everyday life, encouraging us to see
beyond the mundane to the divine tapestry woven into every
moment of our existence. It fosters **Cultivating Wonder
through Childlike Perspective**, reminding us that to truly experience the fullness of life and spirit, we must retain or rediscover
the capacity to look at the world with awe and excitement, much
like children who marvel at everything around them.

In this process, wonder acts as a **Spiritual Catalyst**. It
pushes us toward deeper spiritual engagement, prompting us to

ask questions, seek answers, and dive into the mysteries of God with renewed vigor. This sense of wonder is crucial because it helps us overcome the barriers of routine and skepticism that can cloud our perceptions and dampen our spiritual fires. It challenges us to break free from the **Wonder's Role in Overcoming Cynicism**, ensuring that we never take for granted the beauty and complexity of life and the Creator behind it.

To truly integrate wonder into our lives, it's essential to **Document Moments of Wonder**. Writing down when and how we encounter these moments creates a physical reminder of their impact and reinforces their importance in our lives. This practice not only preserves the memories but also helps us to **Share Wonder with Others**, spreading the infectious joy and awe that comes from recognizing the extraordinary in the ordinary. By sharing, we not only multiply our own experiences of wonder but also ignite the spark of curiosity and awe in others.

However, cultivating this sense isn't always passive; it requires action. **Proactive Cultivation of Wonder** involves seeking out experiences and environments that stir awe and inspiration. Whether it's through nature, art, science, or scripture, actively engaging with sources of wonder ensures that our sense of amazement remains vibrant and ever-present. It transforms everyday experiences and deepens our appreciation for the world and our place within it.

Moreover, **Reflection as a Tool for Appreciating Wonder** is invaluable. By regularly reflecting on past experiences of wonder, we gain a greater appreciation of how these moments shape our understanding and enhance our lives. This reflection can also lead to a more profound **Integration of Wonder into Daily Life**, turning what might otherwise be mundane tasks into opportunities for discovery and joy.

Finally, the pursuit of wonder is an endless journey. It fuels a **Lifelong Curiosity** that drives us to keep exploring, questioning, and learning. This curiosity ensures that our lives never stagnate but continue to expand in knowledge, joy, and appreciation. Wonder not only enhances our spiritual and intellectual growth but also solidifies our connections with others and with God.

REFLECTIVE QUESTIONS

1. When was the last time you truly felt a sense of wonder, and what sparked it?
2. How can engaging with children teach you about maintaining a sense of wonder?
3. What daily activities can you transform into opportunities for wonder?
4. How can documenting your experiences of wonder enhance your spiritual and emotional life?
5. What are some ways to share your experiences of wonder with others to inspire them?

ACTIONABLE STEPS

- **Cultivate Daily Moments of Wonder**: Intentionally incorporate activities into your daily routine that are likely to inspire awe and wonder.
- **Equip Yourself with Tools for Discovery**: Carry a notebook or use a digital app to capture moments of wonder—whether it's something you see, hear, or think.
- **Engage in Community Exploration**: Organize or participate in community events that encourage

exploration and appreciation of the natural world or human creativity.

Journaling Prompt

Reflect on an instance from the past month where you experienced a moment of wonder. Describe the situation, how it made you feel, and what it taught you about the world and your relationship with God. Consider how maintaining a sense of wonder can change your approach to life and spirituality moving forward.

D DESTINY IMAGE

Destiny Image is a prophetic Christian publisher dedicated to empowering believers through Spirit-led messages. Our mission is to equip and inspire individuals to fulfill their God-given destinies by providing transformative resources that resonate with the Charismatic and Pentecostal faith.

We specialize in books, blogs, and back cover copies that reflect prophetic insights, dynamic teachings, and testimonies of faith. Our commitment to fostering spiritual growth and kingdom impact makes Destiny Image a beacon for those seeking to deepen their relationship with God and embrace their calling in the power of the Holy Spirit.